HOW TO DRAW FANTASY ART

WITCHES AND WIZARDS

Steve Beaumont

W

FRANKLIN WATTS

LONDON•SYDNEY

Reprinted in 2008

First published in 2007 by Franklin Watts

Franklin Watts
338 Euston Road
London NW1 3BH

Franklin Watts Australia
Level 17/207 Kent St, Sydney, NSW 2000

Produced by Arcturus Publishing Limited,
26/27 Bickels Yard, 151–153 Bermondsey Street, London SE1 3HA

Artwork and text: Steve Beaumont
Editor: Alex Woolf
Designer: Jane Hawkins

A CIP catalogue record for this book is available from the British Library.

Dewey Decimal Classification Number: 743'.87

ISBN: 978 0 7496 7655 1

Printed in China

Franklin Watts is a division of Hachette Children's Books,
an Hachette Livre UK company.
www.hachettelivre.co.uk

Contents

Introduction

If you've picked up this book, you are probably a big fan of sword-and-sorcery movies, books or games. You may be one of those fans who enjoys the genre so much that you'd like to have a go at creating some magical characters for yourself. If so, this book will help you get started on the right path.

One of the best things about drawing witches, wizards and other fantasy figures is that – apart from the basic rules of anatomy and perspective – there are no other rules. In fantasy art, no one can tell you that a character's nose is too long or her skin is too green – these are products of your imagination and you can draw them exactly as you please!

Witches

Myths and legends describe witches as women who have made a pact with the devil in order to gain magical powers. They are often shown as ugly old crones with long, matted hair, shrieking curses at people. But there are good witches, too. And some can be beautiful. In this book, we'll have a go at drawing a good witch and an evil witch.

Wizards

Wizards are beings who can use superhuman or magical powers to change the world around them. In their human form they usually appear as wise old men. Some wizards, known as druids, use their magic for good purposes. Others, called sorcerers, devote themselves to evil. In this book, we'll be meeting both a druid and a sorcerer.

Equipment

To start with, you'll need the tools of the trade. Decent materials and equipment are essential if you want to produce high-quality illustrations.

Paper

For your practice sketches, buy some cheap A4 or A3 paper from a stationery shop. When practising ink drawing, use line art paper, which can be purchased from an art or craft shop.

For painting with watercolours, use watercolour paper. Most art shops stock a large range of weights and sizes – 250 g/m or 300 g/m is fine.

Pencils

Get a good range of lead pencils ranging from soft (6B) to hard (2H). Hard-leaded pencils last longer and leave fewer smudges on your paper. Soft-leaded ones leave darker marks on the paper and wear down more quickly. 2H pencils are a good medium-range product to start with.

For fine, detailed work, mechanical pencils are ideal. These are available in a range of lead thicknesses, 0.5 mm being a good middle range.

Pens

For inking, use either a ballpoint or a simple dip pen and nib. For colouring, experiment with the wide variety of felt-tips on the market.

Markers

These are very versatile pens that, with practice, can give very pleasing results.

Brushes

Some artists like to use a fine brush for inking line work. This takes a bit more practice to master, but the results can be very satisfying. If you want to try your hand at brushwork, you will need some good-quality sable brushes.

Watercolours and gouache

Most art shops will also stock a wide range of these products from student to professional quality.

Inks

Any good brand will do.

Eraser

There are three types of eraser: rubber, plastic and putty. Try all three to see which you prefer.

INDIAN INK

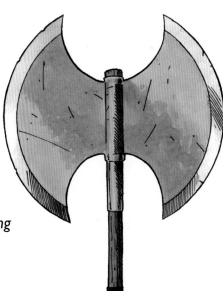

Oh, and you may need something for sharpening your pencils…

Faces

As with all character drawing, so much of the personality of a witch or wizard is to be found in the face, and especially the eyes and mouth. It's therefore worth spending a bit of time honing your techniques in this crucial area.

Constructing the face

The human head generally fits into a square. Note that the nose and chin protrude slightly. It may help to divide the square into quarters. The eyes generally sit halfway above the centre line, with the nose taking up half the depth of the bottom square. Note the alignment of the ears in relation to the eyes and nose. This example is based on a standard-sized head – of course, with fantasy drawing, it may be necessary to adjust this formula.

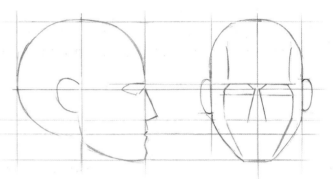

Eyes

These eyes are serious-looking, but not scary. They might sit well on the face of a druid.

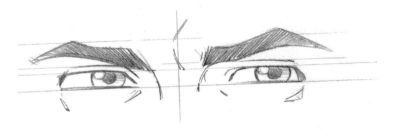

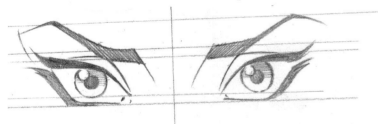

These eyes are clearly feminine, so no prizes for figuring out to whom they belong.

Whoa! These eyes are definitely not inviting you over for dinner, unless of course you happen to be on the menu. These could be right for a sorcerer.

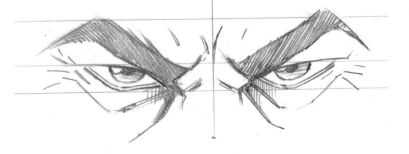

Mouths

Study these simple drawings of mouths. Note how the male and female mouths differ. A simple way of establishing the sex of a character is to keep the mouth of the male simple, without lips (don't worry, this will look fine), and to draw full lips on the female. It also helps to make male characters' mouths bigger than those of females.

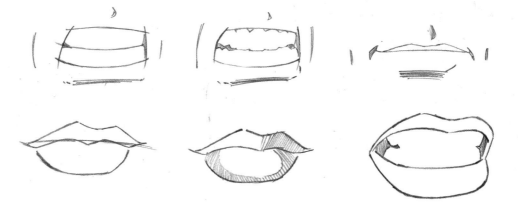

Putting it all together

Now let's try to put together what we've learned and draw a wizard's face. To make it a little more tricky, this one is looking down at a three-quarter angle. When drawing wizards' faces, remember they should be ancient-looking as they will have spent a lifetime devoting themselves to the art of magic. A nice long beard is a good starting point.

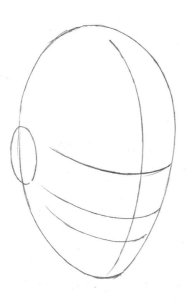

Good Witch

Witches don't have to be ugly, as they can use their powers to make themselves appear very attractive, if not beautiful — like this one here.

Stage 1

The pose of this character is unusual because she will be floating (in fact, appearing from mist) and not standing. Start with a stick figure to establish her basic shape. Note how the lines are drawn to a point at the bottom just above the crystal ball.

Stage 2

Add body shape to the stick figure. The human form can be constructed from geometric shapes such as cylinders and spheres. Use these to create her head, torso and limbs. There is no need for feet because she will only appear solid from the knees up.

Stage 3

Now put in the facial features. Give her large eyes and full lips. Add the outer body form over the geometric shapes.

Stage 4

Now erase the geometric shapes and draw her garments. Dress her in fine, delicate robes.

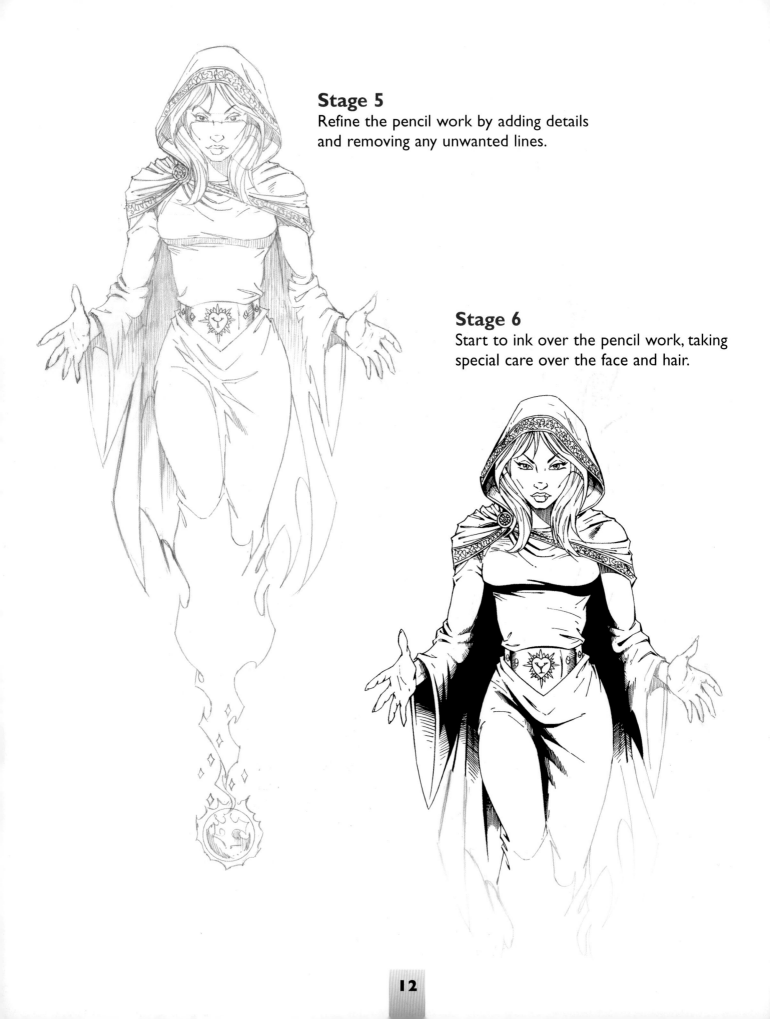

Stage 5
Refine the pencil work by adding details
and removing any unwanted lines.

Stage 6
Start to ink over the pencil work, taking
special care over the face and hair.

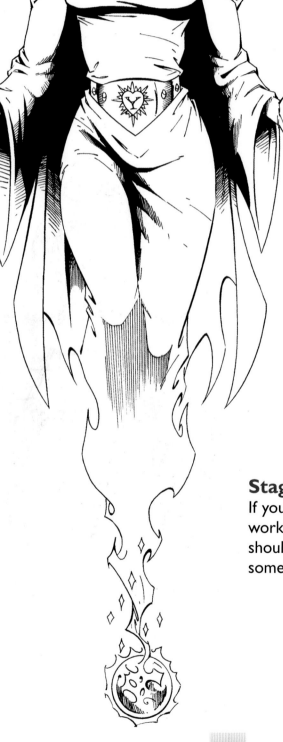

Stage 7
If you've kept the line work nice and crisp, you should end up with something quite dramatic.

Stage 8

You can colour your drawing,
if you like, using marker pens, felt-tips
or watercolours. Lay down each colour
in one continuous wash if you can,
applying the colour as smoothly as
possible. To give depth and shape to
your drawing, apply a second wash in a
darker tone of the same colour range.
Make sure the first coat is completely
dry before applying the second coat.

Evil Witch

Our evil witch should look powerful and scary, with wild hair and outstretched arms, as she summons up the dark forces at her command.

Stage 1
Use the stick figure to create a dynamic pose.

Stage 2
Now apply the geometric shapes, as you did in the previous exercise. Use more slender shapes for a female figure than you would for a male.

Stage 3
Witches are often depicted as nightmarish creatures to be feared, so let's give her a scary face – not necessarily ugly, but definitely scary.

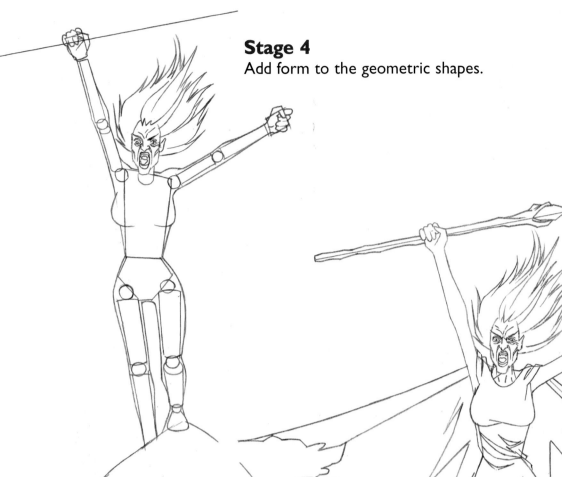

Stage 4
Add form to the geometric shapes.

Stage 5
To add to the witch's nightmarish quality, dress her in tattered black robes that flap around her. Let's also give her a mystical staff for conjuring her black magic. It could a dragon's bone or a twisted branch from a magical tree. Add detail to the mound on which she's standing, so that it begins to form the top of a high rock or mountain.

Stage 6

Give her some bone bracelets and a necklace. Snakes are always a welcome visual aid when creating images of evil so let's place one in her hand, as if she is using it as part of the spell. Such details help to define the witch's evil nature.

Stage 7

Add further details to her face, hair and costume. Give depth to your drawing with shadows and highlights.

Stage 8
Once you've tidied up your pencil work, start adding black ink. You can use a brush or pen, whichever you feel more comfortable with.

Stage 9
If you take enough time and care over the inking, you should end up with a powerful and dramatic illustration.

Stage 10

Giving the witch a pale complexion makes the darker areas of the image, such as the eyes and mouth, more intense. You can make the character even more nightmarish by adding a slight green hue to her skin.

Good Wizard

Druids spend their lives working for the greater good. They are devoted to the pursuit of knowledge, truth and the harnessing of cosmic energy.

Stage 1
Let's start with the basic stick figure.

Stage 2
Apply the geometric shapes around the stick figure.

20

Stage 3

Now give the head some features. Wizards tend to look a bit on the ancient side, so give him a thin, scraggy face and a big, white beard (see pages 8–9 for help with faces). Draw the outer form over the geometric shapes to give a more realistic appearance.

Stage 4

Erase the geometric shapes and add some clothing. Wizards aren't exactly renowned for their cool dress sense – they're too busy mixing potions and casting spells. Long, baggy clothes with a hood and a cape seem to be the standard garb for these guys. Give him a mystical staff and he's ready to begin his incantations.

Stage 5

Now tidy up your pencil drawing, adding
finer details and erasing any unwanted lines or
shading in the areas where shadow or solid
colour will appear. It's better to establish this
now rather than ink in the wrong parts later on,
because ink is harder to correct.

Stage 6

Let's strengthen the pencil outlines
by adding black ink. When inking,
don't be afraid to add extra lines
if you feel that it adds more
interest to the drawing.

Stage 7

Vary the width of the inked lines to accentuate the shadows in the wizard's face and the folds in his clothing.

Stage 8

If you want to colour your drawing, use a mid-range skin tone for the flesh and a light brown for your wizard's clothes.

Evil Wizard

Evil wizards, or sorcerers, use their magic powers to make bad things happen. This particular wizard is definitely not the sort of character you'd want to cross.

Stage 1
As always, we start with the stick figure.

Stage 2
Now add the geometric shapes.

Stage 3

Apply some detail to the face. This guy is evil, so give him narrow, cruel-looking eyes. We'll give him a beard and straggly hair for a more sinister look.

Stage 4

Give the figure a smoother form by drawing over the geometric shapes. Add definition to the hands, which are in the act of conjuring.

Stage 5
To establish more of a contrast between good and evil wizards, we'll dress up this character in darker and more sinister-looking garments than the druid in the previous exercise.

Stage 6
Add further details and shading to your pencil drawing to give your image strength and depth.

Stage 7
Now start to apply the ink to the line work.

Stage 8
Here we have the finished ink drawing of an evil wizard calling up the powers of darkness.

Stage 9

Colour is a useful way of establishing the nature of your character. Dark colours, for example, are commonly used to represent evil in illustration and cinema. As well as using blacks and greys, you could try adding some dark red and green tones.

Glossary

alignment The positioning of different parts of an object, or of several objects, relative to each other.

anatomy The physical structure of a human or other organism.

complexion The quality and colour of the skin, especially of the face.

conjure Perform magic by reciting a spell.

crystal ball A clear solid sphere of glass or rock crystal used to predict the future.

cylinder A shape with straight sides and circular ends of equal size.

druid A good wizard. Also a priest in an ancient religion who worships the forces of nature.

dynamic Full of energy.

facial *adjective* Of the face.

geometric shape Simple shapes, such as cubes, spheres and cylinders.

gouache A mixture of non-transparent watercolour paint and gum.

highlight An area of very light tone in an illustration that provides contrast or the appearance of illumination.

incantation A set of words that are chanted during a magic spell.

mechanical pencil A pencil with replaceable lead that may be advanced as needed.

mystical Something with supernatural or spiritual significance or power.

perspective In drawing, changing the relative size and appearance of objects to allow for the effects of distance.

potion A drink with magical powers.

sable brush An artist's brush made with the hairs of a sable, a small mammal from northern Asia.

sinister Threatening or menacing.

sorcerer A wizard who uses his magic for evil purposes.

sphere An object shaped like a ball.

stick figure A simple drawing of a person with single lines for the torso, arms and legs.

tone Any of the possible shades of a particular colour.

torso The upper part of the human body, not including the head and arms.

versatile Able to be used in many different ways.

watercolour Paint made by mixing pigments (substances that give something its colour) with water.

Further Information

Books

Drawing and Painting Fantasy Figures: From the Imagination to the Page by Finlay Cowan (David and Charles, 2004)

Draw Magical Fantasies: A Step-by-Step Guide by Damon J. Reinagle (Peel Productions, 2002)

How to Draw Fairies and Mermaids by Fiona Watt and Jan McCafferty (illustrator) (Usborne, 2005)

How to Draw Fantasy Characters by Christopher Hart (Watson-Guptill Publications, 1999)

How to Draw Ghosts, Goblins, Witches and other Spooky Characters by Barbara Soloff Levy (Sagebrush, 1999)

How to Draw Wizards, Dragons and other Magical Creatures by Barbara Soloff Levy (Dover Publications, 2004)

Websites

drawsketch.about.com/od/drawfantasyandscifi/tp/imagination.htm
Advice on drawing from the imagination.

elfwood.lysator.liu.se/farp/art.html
An online guide to creating your own fantasy art.

> **Note to parents and teachers:**
>
> Every effort has been made by the publishers to ensure that these websites are suitable for children and contain no inappropriate or offensive material. However, because of the nature of the Internet, it is impossible to guarantee that the contents of these sites will not be altered. We strongly advise that Internet access is supervised by a responsible adult.

Index